Our Terrariums

Our Terrariums

by Herbert H. Wong
and Matthew F. Vessel

illustrated by
Aldren A. Watson

 Addison-Wesley

Science Series for the Young

Level A:
My Ladybug
My Goldfish
Our Tree
Our Terrariums

 **An Addisonian Press Book**

The Addison-Wesley Publishing Company, Inc.
Reading, Massachusetts
Library of Congress catalog card number 69-15805
Printed in the United States of America
First printing

What is that?
That animal. See?
Where?

There it is!
There! In Jean's garden.
Let me get it!

I got it!
What is it?
Let me look!
Jean looks at the animal.
Ed looks, too.

Jean's Dad comes out to see.
He says the animal is a toad.

8

We want to keep our toad.
We want to watch it.

Can we keep it?
Yes, but we must make a home for it.
We can watch it for three or four days.
Then we will let it go.

The toad lives in a garden habitat.
We will make a garden habitat home.
We can make one in a terrarium.

But what can we put in the terrarium?
Jean's Dad says to look in the garden.
What is in it? We look.
There is dirt.
We get some of the dirt.

Jean's Dad says to put some
rocks in the terrarium.
Then Ed puts in lots of dirt.

There are plants in the garden.
Do we want some in our terrarium?
Why, yes.

Jean puts some plants in.
What then?

14

The garden is damp.
So Jean makes the terrarium damp.

Ed puts our toad in.
Then Jean puts a cover
on the terrarium.

16

Why a cover?
So the habitat will not dry out.
And so the toad will not get out.

We have dirt and rocks in our terrarium.
We have plants and our toad.
What now?
We look at the garden.
Animals!
Lots of little animals!
There are earthworms and sowbugs in the garden.

Jean looks under the plants.
She finds three sowbugs and one earthworm.
Ed finds four earthworms.
I find a sowbug.
And a surprise!
Crickets! Big and little crickets!
We put the animals in our terrarium.
Our toad eats one cricket.

It is fun to watch our toad.
But Ed does not want to watch.
He wants to look for new animals.
He goes to the empty lot.

20

And what does he find?
A lizard!

21

Can we keep the lizard, too?
Can we watch it for three or four days?

We put it in our garden terrarium.
But Ed says it does not look right.
Why not?
The lizard did not live in the garden.

22

The lizard was in the empty lot.
The empty lot does not look like the garden.
The garden is damp.
The empty lot is dry.

What can we do?
We can make a new terrarium.
A terrarium for the lizard.
The terrarium will look like the dry empty lot.

24

We put in some rocks.
Then some dirt.
Then some empty-lot plants.

Now in goes the lizard.

Our toad eats animals.
What does a lizard eat?
A lizard eats animals, too.
Lizards eat things like flies.

27

Ed says he can find some fruit flies.
The fruit flies are by some fruit.
So Ed gets the fruit.
He puts some in the terrarium.
The flies will be food for our lizard.

28

Jean puts a cover on the terrarium.
Now the flies can go in or out.
And the lizard cannot get out.

Now we have two terrariums.
But what if Ed finds a new animal some day?
What if Jean does?
What if I find one?
Can we watch the animal in a terrarium?
And then let it go?

Yes, if we make the right habitat.
We can look at where the animal lives.
If our terrarium looks like that, it is right.

Our garden terrarium is right for our toad.
Our empty-lot terrarium is right for the lizard.
We have the right habitats for our animals.

31

About the Authors

Herbert H. Wong is well known as an author of science books for children and teachers, as a science education consultant, and as an educator. He is the Principal of the University of California Laboratory School, Washington Elementary, in Berkeley, California. Dr. Wong is active in many current science curriculum development projects and pilot programs. He holds the Ed.D. from the University of California.

Matthew F. Vessel, Associate Dean of the School of Natural Sciences and Mathematics of San Jose State College, is an author, editor, and consultant, in science and education. He is a Fellow of the American Association for the Advancement of Science. An active member of many other professional science and education societies, Dr. Vessel attended St. Cloud Teachers College and the University of Minnesota. He holds the Ph.D. from Cornell University.

About the Artist

Aldren A. Watson's credits include illustrations for well over a hundred books, eight of which he also wrote. As an illustrator-designer he has worked for major book publishers, industrial firms, magazines, and educational institutions. His work is represented by illustrations, prints, and paintings in public and private collections. An editor of special publishing projects, he continues his design practice, dividing his time between New York and his studio home in Putney, Vermont.